INNER f*cking PEACE

A JOURNAL TO TRANSCEND YOUR BULLSH*T AND BE HAPPY

Cynthia Scher

PETER PAUPER PRESS, INC.
WHITE PLAINS, NEW YORK

THIS BOOK IS DEDICATED TO MY KIDS, NICK AND ELYSSA,
WHO HAVE TAUGHT ME THE VALUE OF APPRECIATING MYSELF,
F BOMBS AND ALL, ON THIS JOURNEY TOWARD INNER FUCKING
PEACE. AND TO MY CAT, ZSA ZSA, THE QUEEN OF LYING AROUND
AND NOT GIVING A FUCK WHAT ANYONE ELSE THINKS.

Images used under license from Shutterstock.com.
Mandala art courtesy of Creative Market.

Designed by Heather Zschock

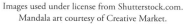

Visit us at www.peterpauper.com

WELCOME,
Beautiful You!

GLAD YOU'RE HERE READY TO GRAB YOUR FAIR SHARE OF INNER F*CKING PEACE! AFTER ALL, YOU DESERVE IT AS MUCH AS ANYONE, DON'T YOU THINK? SO JOIN IN THE FUN!

YOU'RE PROBABLY THINKING, "HOLD ON THERE. YOU'RE TELLING ME I NOT ONLY *DESERVE* INNER PEACE, BUT I'LL HAVE FUN FINDING IT, TOO?!" YOU BET YOUR ASS! SURE, YOU MAY HAVE THOUGHT YOU COULD ONLY CULTIVATE INNER F*CKING PEACE WITH HARD WORK AND DISCIPLINE (DISCIPLINE . . . YUCK), BUT THERE ARE SIMPLE WAYS TO BECOME ONE WITH YOUR HIGHER POWER WITHOUT HAVING TO GET ALL SERIOUS. THINK ABOUT IT: HAVEN'T YOU EVER WONDERED WHY BUDDHA WAS ALWAYS LAUGHING? WELL, NOW YOU GET TO BE IN ON THE JOKE!

YOU WON'T FIND THE USUAL NAMBY-PAMBY BULLSHIT HERE, EITHER. SERIOUSLY, THIS JOURNAL SIMPLY PROVIDES SUGGESTIONS FOR TAKING LITTLE STEPS TO RELEASE THE CRAP AND DOING EASY EXERCISES TO EM-BRACE YOUR HAPPY. JUST FOLLOW THE PROMPTS. YOU CAN EVEN JUMP AROUND OR SKIP RIGHT OVER ANYTHING YOU DON'T LIKE. THERE'S NO WRONG WAY TO DO THIS. BREAK OUT OR BREAK THE RULES! IT'S ALL GOOD. READY TO GET STARTED? LET'S GO FIND YOU SOME BLISS!

Be a rainbow in someone's cloud.

- MAYA ANGELOU

WHEN YOU'RE HAVING SUCH A GREAT DAY THAT YOU
HAVE A LITTLE EXTRA BOUNCE IN YOUR STEP, SHARE SOME
OF YOUR JOY! YOU DON'T HAVE TO GO ALL POLLYANNA
ON SOMEONE'S ASS, BUT JUST DO SOMETHING NICE
THAT'S MEANT TO HELP THEM FEEL GOOD.
(BONUS: YOU'LL FEEL PRETTY DAMN GOOD DOING IT, TOO.)

Think of a time when you felt a little down and someone did something nice for you. Describe what that person did for you and how that changed your day.

Who could use that from you right now? What could you do to help make their day a little brighter?

Even Nuns Want to Change Their Habits Sometimes

YOUR MIND ABHORS A VACUUM. NEXT TIME YOU WANT TO CHANGE A HABIT, MAKE SURE YOU HAVE A NEW ONE TO REPLACE IT WITH. DEVELOPING NEW HABITS WILL HELP KEEP YOU FROM FALLING BACK INTO OLD PATTERNS THAT ARE NO LONGER USEFUL.

Write down one habit you'd like to be rid of.

What's a new (healthy) habit you can develop in its place?

Now keep track of your new habit for the next 100 days. Check off each day you do your new habit:

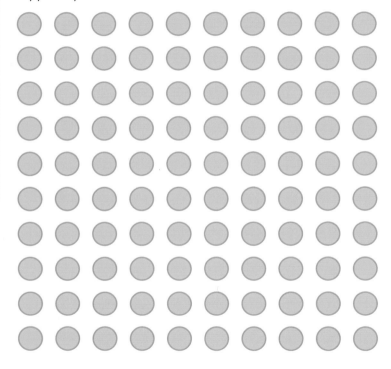

WE ARE WHAT WE REPEATEDLY DO. EXCELLENCE, THEN, IS NOT AN ACT BUT A HABIT.

Will Durant

Mind Meanies

YOU KNOW THOSE VOICES IN YOUR HEAD THAT SAY MEAN THINGS ABOUT YOUR LOOKS, YOUR INTELLIGENCE, OR YOUR CHOICES? THEY'RE TRIGGERING SOME POWERFUL EMOTIONAL REACTIONS BY USING THE EXACT WORDS OF PEOPLE FROM YOUR PAST. SOMETIMES JUST POINTING AT THEM AND LAUGHING IS ENOUGH TO MAKE THEM SHUT UP AND GO AWAY. OR SOMETIMES, IT HELPS TO INVITE THEM TO TEA.

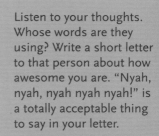

Listen to your thoughts. Whose words are they using? Write a short letter to that person about how awesome you are. "Nyah, nyah, nyah nyah nyah!" is a totally acceptable thing to say in your letter.

We have to learn to be our own
best friends because we fall too
easily into the trap of being our
own worst enemies.

Roderick Thorpe

DOUCHE CANOES
on the Road

YOU CAN BE DRIVING ALONG, CALMLY MINDING YOUR
OWN BUSINESS, AND THEN SOME IDIOT CUTS IN FRONT
OF YOU WITHOUT SIGNALING. WHAT A DOUCHE!
WHO WOULDN'T WANT TO GIVE 'EM THE FINGER? NEXT
TIME THAT HAPPENS, THINK OF DRIVING AS AN ART.
YOU HAVE THE TALENT OF MONET OR REMBRANDT.
THE OTHER DRIVER IS SIMPLY NOT GIFTED,
SO INSTEAD OF THE FINGER, GIVE THEM A LITTLE
SLACK (AND SPACE, DEFINITELY SPACE).

Make a rocking playlist you can sing at top volume next time you feel road rage coming on.

Never underestimate the therapeutic power of driving and listening to very loud music.

UNKNOWN

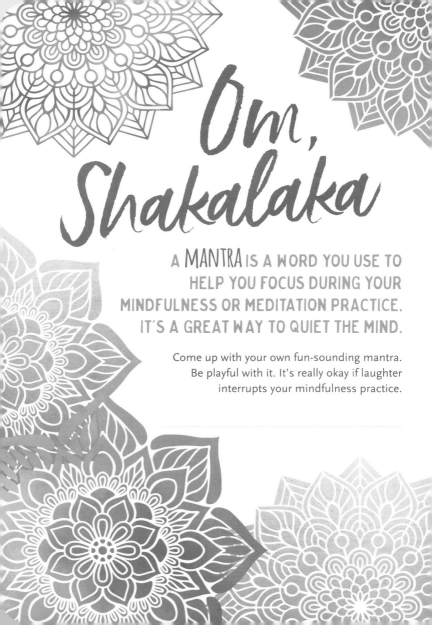

Om, Shakalaka

A MANTRA IS A WORD YOU USE TO HELP YOU FOCUS DURING YOUR MINDFULNESS OR MEDITATION PRACTICE. IT'S A GREAT WAY TO QUIET THE MIND.

Come up with your own fun-sounding mantra. Be playful with it. It's really okay if laughter interrupts your mindfulness practice.

Jot down paths of meditation that you enjoy,
whether it's a sitting practice, walking, mindful eating...
whatever floats your boat.

THE GREAT SONG OF THE THOUSAND VOICES CONSISTED
OF ONE WORD, WHICH WAS OM: PERFECTION.
Hermann Hesse

To Do

1. Clean Up Cat Barf
2. Scoop Up Dog Shit

IT'S TRUE THAT INNER PEACE ISN'T JUST FOR ZEN MASTERS AND ASHRAM ADDICTS. BUT UNLIKE THEM, MOST OF US CAN'T (OR DON'T WANT TO) FORGO ALL OUR RESPONSIBILITIES AND MATERIAL STUFF. HERE'S A LITTLE SECRET: EVEN ZEN MASTERS HAVE SHIT TO DO. SO, CLEAN THAT BARF ON THE CARPET (IT'S NEVER ON THE TILE FLOOR, AM I RIGHT?), AND FIND YOUR PEACE IN THE MIDST OF IT. IT MAY EVEN BE HIDING IN A CLOGGED TOILET!

Think of your least-favorite chores. What can you learn from these chores? Does the cat barf teach you patience toward animals? Does the wine stain on your favorite white shirt teach you the value of simple things (like bleach)? Write about the hidden lessons and gifts of these odious tasks.

CHORE:

HIDDEN GIFT:

CHORE:

HIDDEN GIFT:

CHORE:

HIDDEN GIFT:

CHORE:

HIDDEN GIFT:

*Before enlightenment,
chop wood, carry water.
After enlightenment,
chop wood, carry water.*

ZEN PROVERB

Mondays
GET A BAD RAP

SUNDAY'S HERE. ARE YOU SPENDING HALF OF IT DREADING MONDAY? INSTEAD OF WASTING A PERFECTLY GOOD DAY, USE THE EVENING TO KICK-START YOUR WEEK. PUT FRESH SHEETS ON YOUR BED, FINISH YOUR LAUNDRY, OR MAKE SOME MEALS FOR THE WEEK. THEN BEFORE GOING TO BED, DO SOMETHING GOOD FOR YOURSELF. MEDITATE. TAKE A WARM BATH (WITH SOME SOOTHING LAVENDER). OR DO ANY OTHER FAVORITE PAMPERING ACTIVITY. STARTING A NEW WEEK MIGHT NOT SEEM SO BAD IF YOU CAN ANTICIPATE THAT PAMPER SESSION THE NIGHT BEFORE.

List five things you can do to prep for your week.

1.

2.

3.

4.

5.

How can you pamper yourself on Sunday evenings?

WHEN LIFE GIVES YOU MONDAY, DIP IT IN GLITTER
AND SPARKLE ALL DAY.
Ella Woodward

Castles
IN THE SKY

AS A KID, DID YOU EVER JUST LIE IN THE GRASS WATCHING THE CLOUDS? THEY'D TURN INTO FAMILIAR SHAPES, KIND OF LIKE A RORSCHACH INK BLOT. DO IT AGAIN!

Draw some clouds. Make one of them look like it's floating off the right side of the page, and write something you want to let go of on it. Have another cloud floating onto the page from the left, and write something on it that you want to bring into your life.

Clouds come floating into my life, no longer to carry rain or usher storm, but to add color to my sunset sky.

RABINDRANATH TAGORE

ASSES *and* DUMBASSES

THERE'S SOMETHING ABOUT WATCHING ANIMALS DO CRAZY STUFF THAT'S FUN AND RELAXING. FOR EXAMPLE, I ONCE PUT ON SOME SOUL MUSIC AND DANCED WITH A DONKEY. I WAS LAUGHING THE ENTIRE TIME. SO WAS HE. HE PROBABLY THOUGHT I WAS A DUMBASS.

List three animals that make you laugh.

1. _____

2. _____

3. _____

Turn off that Netflix series and binge-watch a bunch of animal videos instead. Which one was your favorite? Why?

Animals are such agreeable friends —
they ask no questions, they pass no criticisms.

GEORGE ELIOT

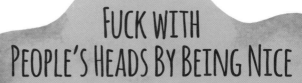

FUCK WITH PEOPLE'S HEADS BY BEING NICE

BEING SNARKY AND EDGY CAN MAKE YOU SEEM COOL, AND IT MIGHT EVEN BE YOUR ENTRY TICKET INTO THE BEST PARTIES. WHAT WOULD HAPPEN IF YOU STARTED ACTING NICE INSTEAD? WOULD EVERYONE'S HEAD EXPLODE?

Pick someone with whom you usually trade barbs. Plan something nice to say instead. Then say it.

What do you think will happen?

Write down your ideas, followed by the actual conversation, here:

Wit is an intermittent fountain; kindness is a perennial spring.

MARIE EBNER-ESCHENBACH

Imagine There's No Country

WE HUMANS HAVE THIS STUPID HABIT OF LABELING "MINE" AS BEST AND "THEIRS" AS LESSER THAN: MY FAMILY, MY TEAM, MY COUNTRY, MY RELIGION, MY RACE, MY GENDER, ETC. RAH FUCKIN' RAH! BUT THE TRUTH IS, DECIDING WHO IS ONE OF US AND WHO ISN'T IS REALLY JUST BULLSHIT.

TAKE A TIP FROM JOHN LENNON AND IMAGINE THAT ALL THE DIFFERENCES YOU USED TO SEE BETWEEN "ME" AND "THEM" NO LONGER EXIST. ARE YOU ABLE TO DO IT?

WE BUILD TOO MANY WALLS AND NOT ENOUGH BRIDGES.

Joseph Fort Newton

Write down how you feel as you do this exercise in imagining. Be honest.

Is there any group or individual you have trouble accepting into your world? Why?

THERE'S GOLD IN THEM THERE HILLS

NATURE IS SO COOL, ISN'T IT? IT CAN CALM YOU DOWN AND GET YOU AWAY FROM ALL THE LUNATICS AROUND YOU. IT CAN GRAB YOUR ATTENTION AND LEAVE YOU FEELING COMPLETELY PRESENT. HELL, IT CAN EVEN BE A PORTAL TO SPIRITUAL AWARENESS!

Go outside and find a tree. Touch it. Hug it if you want to. Mostly, just ask it questions and listen to the answers.

Write your Q&A below.

Keep close to Nature's heart...and break clear away, once in a while, and climb a mountain or spend a week in the woods. Wash your spirit clean.

JOHN MUIR

Dropping a Load

FEELING BLOATED? IT'S PROBABLY ALL THOSE RESENT-
MENTS YOU'RE CARRYING AROUND IN YOUR GUT. BUT THAT
BITCH FROM EIGHTH GRADE PROBABLY DESERVES THE BILE
THAT ACCUMULATES WHENEVER YOU THINK OF HER. LET IT
GO? FORGIVE HER? NO WAY! WHY SHOULD YOU LET HER (OR
ANYONE ELSE WHO'S DONE YOU WRONG) OFF THE HOOK?
HERE'S WHY. FORGIVENESS ISN'T ABOUT SAYING YOU'RE
OKAY WITH WHAT THEY DID. IN FACT, IT'S NOT ABOUT
THEM AT ALL. IT'S MORE LIKE A GOOD DETOX.

List the people who still affect your bowels. How long ago did they do
you wrong?

_Resentment is like drinking poison and waiting
for the other person to die._

UNKNOWN

How would it feel if you could be rid of the effect they continue to have on you?

How do you think your resentment affects them? (Hint: It probably doesn't; it only hurts you.)

DUMB SHIT YOU'VE DONE, STUPID PEOPLE YOU'VE KNOWN — A WASTE OF TIME OR FODDER FOR YOUR NEXT EPISODE OF *My Crazy Life*?

If your life were a sitcom, what would it be called?

What actor would play you in the starring role?

Pick a crazy-ass thing that you've been involved in. Summarize it as if you were telling someone about an episode of an off-the-wall comedy. (Don't forget the laugh track!)

It's good to be able to laugh at yourself and the problems you face in life.

TEGAN QUIN

~~EAT, CRAP, AND EXERCISE~~
Eat Crap and Exercise

WITH OR WITHOUT THE PUNCTUATION, IT ALL COMES DOWN TO KNOWING THE CONSEQUENCES OF YOUR "NEGATIVE" ACTIONS AND BALANCING THEM WITH "POSITIVE" ONES. INGEST CRAP AND BURN IT OFF (OR EXCRETE IT). TAKE IN AND GIVE AWAY. YIN AND YANG. SO NEXT TIME YOU DO SOMETHING YOU THINK OF AS "BAD," DON'T BEAT YOURSELF UP. JUST BALANCE IT WITH SOMETHING "GOOD."

In the left-hand column on the opposite page, use a pencil or black pen to list some things you do that you beat yourself up about.

In the right-hand column, use colored markers or sparkly gel pens to list the things you can do to offset each thing you listed in the left-hand column.

I TAKE CRAP IN WHEN I...	I CAN BALANCE IT WITH...

IF YOU TAKE THE YIN-YANG, IT HAS A PIECE OF THE
OTHER INSIDE ITSELF. YOU CAN'T BE TOO MUCH
OF ONE THING AND BE BALANCED.

Shannon Lee

WHY ARE *They* SO DAMN LUCKY?!

DID YOU EVER WISH YOU HAD SOMEONE ELSE'S LIFE? HERE'S A BIG FAT SECRET: THEY HAVE PROBLEMS, TOO—OR THEY WILL. SHIT HAPPENS TO EVERYONE.

If you really, really, REALLY want something they have, think about how it would change your life, both the positives and the negatives. Write them down.

Still want it? If so, make a list below of every step it would take for you to achieve the same thing. Don't leave out any steps.

1.
2.
3.
4.
5.
6.
7.
8.
9.
10.

Look at the first step. Are you willing to do it?

NO ·····▶ *It's not as important as you thought it was, so STOP HERE. Why envy something you're not excited enough to work for? Go be you.*

YES ··▶ *If you really are motivated to do it, then get off your ass and do it already!*

Cross it off your list when you've completed the step.

Move on to the next step. Rinse and repeat until you reach a step you don't want to do or until you get what you want. Either way, HOORAY! You have the life you want!

UPTIGHT AND OUTTA SIGHT:
Breathing

AREN'T LUNGS AMAZING? THOSE POCKET-FILLED SUCKERS (NO PUN INTENDED) JUST KEEP INFLATING AND DEFLATING LIKE A PAIR OF TIRELESS BALLOONS. NO WONDER IT'S SO EASY TO TAKE 'EM FOR GRANTED! WE OFTEN FORGET TO BREATHE WHEN WE'RE STRESSED, WHICH IS KIND OF IRONIC SINCE BREATHING TAKES NO THOUGHT TO DO RIGHT!

Next time you're feeling uptight, inhale deeply on a count of 4 and exhale on a count of 6. Then do a count of 6 in and 10 out. Slowing your breathing will help calm you down.

When people ask me what the most important thing is in life, I answer: Just breathe.

YOKO ONO

Felt stressed by: _____

Breathed deeply ☐

How I felt after: ....

....

Felt stressed by: _____

Breathed deeply ☐

How I felt after: ....

....

Felt stressed by: _____

Breathed deeply ☐

How I felt after: ....

....

Felt stressed by: _____

Breathed deeply ☐

How I felt after: ....

....

Felt stressed by: _____

Breathed deeply ☐

How I felt after: ....

....

Mentors AND Wiseguys

EXPECTING PEARLS FROM AN OYSTER MAKES SENSE, RIGHT? BUT IF YOU OPEN A CLAM THINKING IT'S AN OYSTER, YOU'LL NEVER GET MORE THAN A PILE OF SAND.

IT'S THE SAME THING WITH GUIDES, TEACHERS, AND GURUS. YOU CAN GET SOME REAL PEARLS OF WISDOM FROM SOMEONE WITH MORE EXPERIENCE WHOSE INTENTIONS ARE HONORABLE. BUT SOME ARE JUST LIKE CLAMS (NO OFFENSE TO CLAMS). INSTEAD OF BEING MENTORS THEY'RE WISEGUYS, AND THEY'RE FULL OF SAND—OR SHIT. THE TRICK IS TO KNOW AN OYSTER FROM A CLAM.

HOW TO TELL AN OYSTER FROM A CLAM

For each description below, put a checkmark in the column marked "oyster" if you think it's a sign of a good mentor, or "clam" if you think you'll only get sand from that relationship. Answers are at the end.

	OYSTER (Mentor)	CLAM (Wiseguy)
1. You've been specially chosen, but you have to swear to secrecy.		
2. Recruiting others is a requirement of continuing to learn from them.		
3. They encourage you to check in with your own intuition.		
4. They teach you ways to find your own truth.		
5. They practice what they teach.		
6. They found you; you didn't find them. They tell you it's fate.		
7. They suggest ways to integrate what you learn into your own life.		
8. They want you to give up your life and all your material possessions to them or their organization.		
9. For some reason, you often feel guilty when you don't follow their teachings.		
10. They don't judge you—even when you do stupid things.		

Answers: Oyster = 3, 4, 5, 7, 10 Clam = 1, 2, 6, 8, 9

Ya Got a Little Smudge?

I'm talking about the verb kind of "smudge," whereby you light sage or incense and use the sweet-smelling smoke to clear out the slimy energy in your home or personal aura. Got a sensitive nose? There are other ways to to get rid of energetic slime. You can use drumming, rattling, or a singing bowl. Put a black tourmaline stone or a bowl of salt in a corner of the room, or spray some salt water or lavender water around. For personal de-sliming, take a salt water bath, spray yourself, or wear tourmaline jewelry.

Take a moment to write about your adventures in energy clearing.

Keep only those things that spark joy and discard the rest.

MARIE KONDO

Decide, THEN ENJOY THE RIDE!

DO YOU DRIVE YOURSELF NUTS WITH INDECISION?
EVEN INDECISION ABOUT INCONSEQUENTIAL THINGS LIKE
CHOOSING BETWEEN OREOS OR CHIPS AHOY CAN BE PEACE
ZAPPERS. HERE'S A TRICK MY SON'S DAD USED TO USE
WITH HIM: FLIP A COIN. IF THE OUTCOME FEELS OKAY,
GO WITH IT. IF IT DISAPPOINTS, CHOOSE THE OTHER ONE
AUTOMATICALLY. MANY DECISIONS WON'T GIVE YOU 100
PERCENT OF WHAT YOU WANT ANYWAY. BUT THEY WILL ALL
GIVE YOU EXPERIENCES TO LEARN FROM, SO YOU MAY AS
WELL MAKE A DECISION AND THEN ENJOY THE RIDE—BUMPS,
POTHOLES, AND ALL.

In any moment of decision, the best thing you can do is the right thing, the next best thing is the wrong thing, and the worst thing you can do is nothing.

UNKNOWN

Look back on a difficult decision you once made. Regardless of whether you think it was a "good" or "bad" decision, what were some things you got out of the choice you made? What did you learn?

Codependency
WELCOME MAT

WHEN'S THE LAST TIME YOU INCLUDED YOURSELF ON YOUR LIST OF PEOPLE NEEDING CARETAKING? IF YOU CAN'T REMEMBER OR IF THAT SOUNDS SELFISH, YOU'VE PROBABLY GOT A LITTLE (OR A LOT) OF CODEPENDENT TENDENCIES. CUT IT OUT! BEING OF SERVICE DOESN'T MEAN ALWAYS DOING FOR OTHERS AT YOUR OWN EXPENSE. EVEN YOUNG CHILDREN CAN DO SOME THINGS FOR THEMSELVES, AND ELDERLY PARENTS MAY HAVE TO ACCEPT THAT A 'STRANGER' WILL BE TAKING YOUR PLACE TO CLEAN THEIR HOUSE.

Daring to set boundaries is about having the courage to love ourselves, even when we risk disappointing others.

BRENE BROWN

What are you afraid would happen if you weren't always there to take care of everyone else? How do you think they would react? How would you feel saying "no"?

Pissed Off?
SUCK IT UP AND VENT IT

DON'T YOU JUST HATE IT WHEN YOU TELL SOMEONE HOW PISSED OFF YOU ARE AND THEY TELL YOU TO JUST "SUCK IT UP"? WELL, FORTUNATELY, THAT'S NOT WHAT I'M TALKING ABOUT HERE. I'M TALKING ABOUT THE KIND YOU DO WITH A VACUUM CLEANER. NEXT TIME YOU NEED TO UNLOAD THAT ANGER ENERGY COLLECTING IN YOUR BODY, DO SOMETHING PRODUCTIVE LIKE CLEANING THE HOUSE OR WEEDING THE GARDEN. (HEY, IT'S BETTER THAN THROWING A ROCK THROUGH SOMEONE'S WINDOW!)

GOING THROUGH SOME CRAPPUCCINO?

TRY A LITTLE VENTI.

When you're done sucking it up, you can vent. Unload what you'd like to say below—NOT in an email or text message (way too easy to hit "Send"). And definitely not on social media.

In times of great stress and adversity, it's always best to keep busy, to plow your anger and your energy into something positive.

LEE IACOCCA

Vacation Make-Believe

WHEN MY KIDS WERE LITTLE, I'D SOMETIMES TAKE THEM TO OUR LOCAL BEACH ON A WARM SUMMER DAY FOR A PICNIC. IT MAY NOT HAVE BEEN THE FRENCH RIVIERA, BUT IT SURE WAS GOOD FOR MY SOUL TO GET A MAKE-BELIEVE VACAY.

A vacation is what you take when you can no longer take what you've been taking.

EARL WILSON

Describe one of your favorite vacation spots. Pick one aspect of it you can recreate close to home. What can you use at home to create that perfect vacation feel?

Dear Blue People

IN A *Twilight Zone* EPISODE, EVERY MINUTE IS CONSTRUCTED
ANEW BY BLUE PEOPLE AS A SEPARATE WORLD FOR HUMANS
TO LIVE IN, THEN DISASSEMBLED TO MAKE WAY FOR THE NEXT
MINUTE/WORLD. THIS EXPLAINED WHY YOUR KEYS MIGHT NOT BE
SOMEWHERE YOU SWORE YOU HAD PUT THEM. (YEAH, EVEN THE
BLUE PEOPLE SCREW UP.) WITH OR WITHOUT BLUE PEOPLE, EACH
MOMENT CAN BE AN OPPORTUNITY TO START ANEW.

CHANGE WILL NOT COME IF
WE WAIT FOR SOME OTHER
PERSON OR IF WE WAIT
FOR SOME OTHER TIME. WE
ARE THE ONES WE'VE BEEN
WAITING FOR.
BARACK OBAMA

If you could tell the Blue People to take a slight detour in one upcoming moment, what would you ask them to change? What's stopping you from creating a new moment yourself?

BLACK and WHITE or GRAY All Over?

SOME PEOPLE NATURALLY SEE THE WORLD IN BLACK AND WHITE. THEY DON'T SEE ALL THE SHADES OF GRAY. IT CAN BE SO ANNOYING TO TRY TO CONVINCE THEM THAT WHAT THEY THINK IS TRUE ISN'T ALWAYS! GUESS WHAT? WE ALL HAVE ENTRENCHED BELIEFS—YEAH, EVEN YOU. SO WHAT HAPPENS WHEN YOU COME UP AGAINST SOMEONE WHO DOESN'T AGREE? DO YOU DIG YOUR HEELS IN DEEPER?

What's one belief you have that no one can convince you isn't absolutely true?

Pretend you have the opposite belief. Write down five things that refute your current belief.

Write a conversation between yourself and this alternate you with the opposite belief. What happens?

There's so much gray to every story—
nothing is so black and white.

LISA LING

The World Doesn't Have to Suck

YEAH, A LOT OF THINGS IN THE WORLD DO SEEM TO SUCK. YET SOME PEOPLE DON'T APPEAR TO NOTICE. WHAT'S THEIR SECRET? MAYBE THEY CHOOSE TO THINK DIFFERENTLY ABOUT THINGS. SIMPLE AS THAT.

List three things in your life that suck.

1.

2.

3.

Now write a different way to think about them that's more positive.

Change your thoughts, and you change your world.
NORMAN VINCENT PEALE

No News Is
GOOD NEWS
for Your Soul

THE NEWS CAN MAKE YOU WANT TO GO CRAWL INTO A HOLE. SO MUCH BAD SHIT HAPPENS ALL THE TIME. BUT IF YOU DON'T PAY ATTENTION, YOU FEEL UNINFORMED. AND BE HONEST: DOESN'T IT GIVE YOU A BIT OF A RUSH WHEN YOU'RE THE FIRST ONE TO TELL OTHERS ABOUT THE LATEST POLITICAL SCANDAL OR CELEBRITY BREAKUP?

Go on a five-day news fast. If you're feeling bold, go on a total media fast. After you've done it, describe the experience.

Bad news travels at the speed of light; good news travels like molasses.

TRACY MORGAN

Candle-ICIOUS DOWNTIME

CANDLELIGHT IS LIKE A GLOWING "AHHHHH."
WHETHER FOR A SPECIAL DINNER, A SOOTHING BATH,
OR A DEEP MEDITATION, LIGHTING CANDLES INSTANTLY
CHANGES A ROOM'S ENERGY. SO GET YOUR PEACE
ON WITH A CANDLE. OR MAKE THAT TWO.

Stare into the flame of a candle and ask it for wisdom. What did it tell you?

When your soul is looking for you, light a candle on its path.

RUMI

DAMN

THERE'S NO ONE LEFT TO BLAME

EVERYONE FUCKS UP, BUT WE HATE TO ADMIT IT
WHEN WE'RE THE FUCKER UPPERS. SO WE POINT
FINGERS INSTEAD OF OWNING UP TO OUR MISTAKES.

Think of a time you blamed someone else for your fuck-up.
What did you do? Why did you blame it on someone else?
What do you think would have happened if you'd owned your
part?

it's your fault it's your fault

> *A man can fail many times, but he isn't a failure until he begins to blame someone else.*
>
> John Burroughs

BITE SIZES

GIANT COOKIES ARE THE BEST, ESPECIALLY WARM OUT OF THE OVEN. TOP 'EM OFF WITH A BIG HONKIN' SCOOP OF ICE CREAM AND SOME CHOCOLATE SYRUP AND THEY'RE FUCKING AMAZING! BETCHA CAN'T SHOVE AN ENTIRE ONE IN YOUR MOUTH IN JUST ONE BITE, THOUGH.

SAME THING WITH GOALS. YOU CAN ONLY GET THROUGH THEM ONE BITE AT A TIME. SO BREAK THEM DOWN, AND TAKE YOUR TIME SAVORING EACH BITE. AVOID GETTING SICK BY NOT TAKING ON TOO MUCH AT A TIME.

WRITE DOWN A GOAL, EVEN A SIMPLE ONE.

NOW, BREAK YOUR GOAL DOWN INTO NUMBERED STEPS, AND CHECK OFF EACH STEP AS YOU DO IT.

☐ 1.

☐ 2.

☐ 3.

☐ 4.

☐ 5.

☐ 6.

☐ 7.

YOU DID IT! DO TELL:

No Regrets

A LOT OF COOL THINGS ARE SCARY AS FUCK TO DO! SO WHAT? DO THEM ANYWAY. AS THE SAYING GOES, IT'S NOT WHAT WE **DO** THAT WE REGRET, BUT WHAT WE **DON'T** DO.

WE'RE NOT HERE TO HIDE UNDER FEARS. WE'RE HERE TO DO COOL SHIT DESPITE THEM.

SHARON PEARSON

Write down some things you've always wanted to do.

Now pick one and go do it! (Bring a friend along if it helps. Fear loves company, too.) Report back below.

FAKE IT 'TIL YOU MAKE IT

DO YOU WISH YOU WERE MORE CONFIDENT? MORE ADVENTUROUS? MORE COMPASSIONATE? PRETEND THAT YOU ARE. YOU DON'T HAVE TO BELIEVE IT. YOU JUST HAVE TO BE AN ACTOR. IF YOU WISH YOU WERE MORE OF AN ACTOR, FAKE THAT, TOO.

I WISH I WERE MORE:

_____

I AGREE TO TAKE ON THAT ROLE AS IF I ALREADY WERE.

SIGNED:

_____

Sure, pledging is easy, but how can you go about faking that?

How's that working for you? Does it feel fake or transformative? Or a little of both?

My fake plants died because I did not pretend to water them.

MITCH HEDBERG

Real Life vs. Reality TV

AH, REALITY TV. WATCHING A BUNCH OF DWEEBS SAY
ASININE THINGS TO OTHER DWEEBS SURE CAN MAKE
YOU FEEL BETTER ABOUT YOUR LIFE! YOU CAN ALSO USE IT
AS A REMINDER THAT DRAMA DOESN'T BENEFIT ANYONE.
IT'S ENTERTAINING, MAYBE, BUT IT USUALLY DOESN'T
MAKE YOUR WORLD PEACEFUL.

How do you create drama in your life?

What can you do differently to trim away some of your real-life reality TV experiences?

There cannot be a crisis next week. My schedule is already full.
HENRY KISSINGER

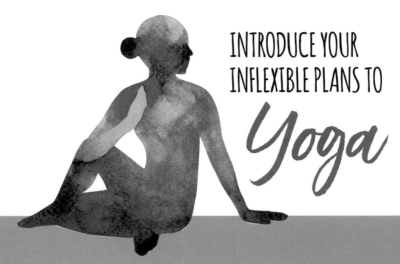

INTRODUCE YOUR INFLEXIBLE PLANS TO *Yoga*

PLANS AND SCHEDULES CAN HELP YOU STAY ORGANIZED. BUT WHEN YOU PLAN OUT EVERYTHING IN YOUR LIFE AND DON'T ALLOW SOME FLEXIBILITY, YOU CAN FIND YOURSELF REALLY DISAPPOINTED WHEN THE PLAN DOESN'T GO— WELL—THE WAY YOU PLANNED. PLUS YOU MAY MISS OUT ON GREAT NEW EXPERIENCES THAT SHOW UP UNEXPECTEDLY. SO BE FLEXIBLE AND LEAVE ROOM FOR SPONTANEITY.

When is the last time you did something spontaneous? What was it like?

Write down some plans you've been rigidly adhering to. How can you add some flexibility?

ADJUST THE COLOR,
Debbie Downer!

HAVE YOU EVER NOTICED HOW EVERYTHING LOOKS MORE WASHED OUT WHEN YOU'RE FEELING LOW, BUT ALL BRIGHT AND SHINY WHEN YOU'RE FEELING GOOD? AND CONVERSELY, IF YOU ARE IN A BLEAK ENVIRONMENT (THINK GRAY CUBICLE), YOU FEEL A BIT LESS ENTHUSIASTIC THAN IF YOU'RE IN A COLORFUL SPACE. I DON'T MEAN PSYCHEDELIC, HEADACHE-INDUCING COLORFUL. JUST ENOUGH TO ADD SOME PIZZAZZ. IF YOU'RE FEELING A LITTLE DOWN OR HAVE A DEPRESSINGLY BLAND SPACE, BRING IN SOME COLOR—FLOWERS OR A BRIGHT WALL HANGING WILL DO. SEE HOW IT AFFECTS YOUR MOOD. FOR A LITTLE EXTRA KICK, GET ONE OF THOSE LED LIGHTBULBS THAT CHANGE COLORS.

COLOR THE MANDALA TO THE RIGHT WITH CRAYONS OR MARKERS.

The whole point is to live life and be— to use all the colors in the crayon box.

RU PAUL

Sacred Silliness

WHEN IS THE LAST TIME YOU HAD A FULL-OUT BELLY LAUGH? IT'S NOT ONLY GOOD FOR YOUR SOUL, BUT IT'S ALSO GOOD FOR YOUR BODY, ACCORDING TO THE MAYO CLINIC. HERE ARE SOME SILLY AND NOT-SO-SILLY WAYS TO GET LAUGHING:

- MAKE A DATE TO GO TO THE LOCAL COMEDY CLUB.

- DO CARTWHEELS, PLAY ON SWINGS, OR CLIMB MONKEY BARS WITH FRIENDS.

- WATCH A STUPID-FUNNY MOVIE. (MEL BROOKS MOVIES FIT THE BILL.)

- GET TOGETHER WITH A FRIEND WHO ALWAYS MAKES YOU LAUGH.

- WATCH BABY ANIMALS PLAY.

- GO SLEDDING IN WINTER OR TO AN AMUSEMENT PARK IN SUMMER.

- EAVESDROP ON A CONVERSATION AMONG TODDLERS.

Never stay up on the barren heights of cleverness, but come down into the green valleys of silliness.

LUDWIG WITTGENSTEIN

PICK ONE, OR COME UP WITH YOUR OWN...
AND GO DO THEM!

List these silly things below. Whenever something works, mark it so you know what to go back to the next time you need a laugh.

AND NOW A WORD FROM YOUR SPONSORS...

PUT ON YOUR CREATIVE THINKING CAP, AND WRITE AN AD ABOUT SOME ASPECT OF YOURSELF. WHY WOULD PEOPLE WANT TO 'BUY' YOU? (EGO ISN'T THE ENEMY. A LITTLE SELF-APPRECIATION CAN LIFT YOU UP.)

List your three best qualities:

1.

2.

3.

Use your graphic design skills (and some colored pens or pencils) to create an eye-catching ad for yourself:

Your most important sale in life is to sell yourself to yourself.

MAXWELL MALTZ

DE-Nile RIVER

WE ALL CARRY AROUND A BUNCH OF DEFENSE MECHANISMS (DENIAL, REPRESSION, PROJECTION, ETC.) THAT MAY HAVE HAD A REAL PURPOSE AT ONE TIME BUT THAT NO LONGER SERVE US. IF YOU CAN FIT THEM IN YOUR POCKET, NO BIG DEAL. BUT IF YOU'RE LUGGING AROUND A SUITCASE FULL OF EXPIRED DEFENSES, YOU GOTTA LET THAT SHIT GO! THE PROBLEM IS THAT MOST DEFENSE MECHANISMS HAVE A LIFESPAN THAT'S WAY LONGER THAN THEIR USEFULNESS.

People choose to shut themselves off and build a load of defense mechanisms and not let anybody in because it's easier that way. You don't get hurt, and there's less risk involved if you build this hard shell.

EMMA MACKEY

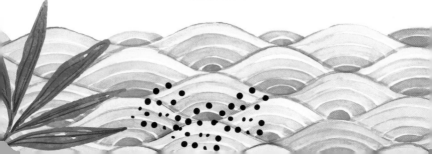

What are some of your defense mechanisms? Write them on the suitcase below, then toss them in the river!

GUIDED MEDICATIONS
(aka Peace Pills)

WOULDN'T IT BE GREAT IF ANYTIME YOU GOT STRESSED OUT
YOU COULD JUST POP A PEACE PILL? WELL, OKAY,
IT DOES EXIST. IT'S CALLED XANAX. BUT I MEAN MORE LIKE
A NATURAL QUICK FIX. HERE ARE SOME OF MY FAVORITE
FIVE-MINUTE FIXES. CIRCLE THE ONES YOU'VE USED.
PUT A STAR NEXT TO THOSE YOU'D LIKE TO TRY.

Deep breathing

Dancing

Running

Reading

Screaming into a pillow

Walking outside barefoot

Jumping up and down

Stretching

Listening to a short guided meditation

Listening to heavy metal

Journaling

Petting a cat, dog, ferret, horse, penguin

MAKE UP YOUR OWN!

IF YOU'RE OUT OF IDEAS FOR THE MOMENT, TAKE A QUICK MEDITATIVE BREATHER
RIGHT NOW BY COLORING THE FLOWERS ON THE NEXT PAGE.

HELP!
I'm Stuck and I Can't Get Up!

DO YOU EVER ENGAGE IN MINDLESS ACTIVITIES THAT

... KEEP YOUR ASS GLUED TO THE COUCH?

... TAKE AWAY YOUR ABILITY TO CHOOSE WHEN TO STOP?

... LEAVE YOU WONDERING WHERE YOUR DAY WENT?

IF SO, YOU NEED TO INSTALL THE ADT (ASS DE-STUCKIFIER TECHNIQUE) EMERGENCY ALERT NETWORK. HERE'S HOW IT WORKS .....▶

1.

Engage three or more friends to be part of your ADT Emergency Alert Network. List them here.

KICK-ASS FRIENDS:

_____

_____

_____

_____

WHEN YOU KILL TIME,
REMEMBER THAT IT HAS
NO RESURRECTION.

Unknown

2.

Before engaging in a mind-less activity, text or call a name in the Network. If they are unavailable, go to the next name. Continue until you find an available Network member.

3.

Inform that member of your time limit for engaging in the mindless activity.

4.

Text or call the member when your time is up. If you haven't called within five minutes of the specified end time, they will call you to make sure you're okay. If you're stuck and you can't get up, they will go into emergency mode and talk you through the disengagement process, whatever that might be. They're *your* friends, so they should know how to kick your ass.

How many times have you used this system so far? Keep a tally.

As handy as the Network may be, what are things that you can do to destick your ass *before* you need the ADT?

The Invisible (Wo)Man

DO YOU EVER FEEL INVISIBLE, LIKE NO ONE EVEN NOTICES WHETHER YOU'RE THERE OR NOT? IT CAN MAKE YOU FEEL LIKE SHIT. BUT JUST LIKE INVISIBLE INK, THERE ARE BENEFITS TO BEING SEEN ONLY BY THE PEOPLE WHO KNOW HOW TO UNCOVER YOUR HIDDEN BEAUTY. LEARN TO APPRECIATE THE BENEFITS OF BEING INVISIBLE.

What might be some benefits of being invisible?

How might you use your invisibility to your advantage? For example, you could use it to eavesdrop on a bus stop conversation as inspiration for your screenplay dialogue.

Write a scenario where your invisibility comes in handy.

*I just think that, for my particular personality,
feeling slightly invisible is always a help.*
JENNIFER EGAN

DON'T BE A DRIED UP LIZARD

HAVING LOTS OF STUFF: IS IT THE AMERICAN DREAM OR THE AMERICAN NIGHTMARE? MORE STUFF MEANS MORE TO KEEP TRACK OF, MORE TO DUST, AND MORE SHIT YOU CAN'T FIND BECAUSE IT'S SOMEWHERE IN A PILE OF OTHER SHIT. I HAD A PILE OF SHIT IN A CORNER FOR A YEAR. WHEN I FINALLY DEALT WITH IT, I FOUND A DRIED UP LIZARD UNDERNEATH IT. POOR LITTLE GUY COULDN'T FIND ITS WAY OUT OF ALL MY SHIT! DO YOU WANT TO END UP LIKE A DRIED UP LIZARD? I DIDN'T THINK SO! START UNLOADING. GET A FRIEND TO HELP YOU UNLOAD IF YOU CAN'T DO IT BY YOURSELF.

Put a check in the box of each true statement:

☐ Having lots of shit is a status symbol for me.

☐ I deserve to have all my stuff.

☐ I'd be lost without my stuff.

☐ My stuff gives me comfort.

☐ My stuff overwhelms me.

☐ I ignore all that stuff.

☐ I can't deal with organizing my stuff.

☐ My stuff has sentimental value.

Now that you've faced the *why* behind your stash, it's time to cut it down. For everything you marked true, write down a counterpoint that argues that, no, you really do need to cut down your clutter collection:

Now for the hard part. **UNCLUTTER YOUR LIFE!** Go through your stuff. Ask yourself if you *really* need each item, then for every item you're not too sure about, toss it or put it in a box to donate.

To keep yourself on task, divide your stuff up into categories of things you need to go through (clothes, books, etc.) and make a checklist below. Check off each category you've powered through, and then when everything's either tossed or taken away, sit back and relax with a drink in your newly decluttered space.

- [ ]
- [ ]
- [ ]
- [ ]
- [ ]
- [ ]
- [ ]
- [ ]

ENJOY THE RIDE

PERFECTION IS SO OVERRATED. IT'S A PAIN IN THE ASS TO YOU AND TO THE PEOPLE AROUND YOU, AND IT'S IMPOSSIBLE TO ACHIEVE. INVITE YOUR IMPERFECTIONS TO SIT SHOTGUN. YOU JUST MIGHT ENJOY THE RIDE A LITTLE MORE!

Pick two areas in which you're a perfectionist and write them below.

1.

2.

Instead of trying to make your life perfect, give yourself the freedom to make it an adventure, and go ever upward.

DREW HOUSTON

Think about how your life could be more fun if you chose "good enough" instead of "perfect." What can you do to remind yourself that good enough is good enough?

DOGMAS AND DIARRHEA

WE HUMANS HAVE A NEED TO BELONG. IT HELPS US FEEL LIKE WE AREN'T JUST STANDING HERE ON A BIG FUCKING ROCK CIRCLING AROUND AND AROUND A GIANT BALL OF GAS WITH NO PURPOSE. BUT SOMETIMES THAT NEED LEADS US TO TRUST IN A PARTICULAR GROUP MORE THAN IN OURSELVES. SO YEAH, BECOME PART OF A GROUP IF IT JIBES WITH WHO YOU ARE. BUT IF SOME PART OF ITS DOGMA LEAVES YOU WITH THAT UNCOMFORTABLE PRE-DIARRHEA GURGLE IN YOUR GUT, TRUST YOUR GUT.

All of us are living with dogmas that we accept as truths. When one of these is overturned, there's an initial gasp, soon followed by a rush of exhilaration.

DEEPAK CHOPRA

Make a list of the groups you belong to, both formally and informally. (Remember to include your family, too.) Which of their beliefs do you agree with? Which do you disagree with? Are you allowed to disagree? If not, why do you think that is? What would happen if you questioned that belief out loud? Try it and see.

DIVING INTO RABBIT HOLES

HAVE YOU EVER LOVED WORKING ON A PROJECT OR ACTIVITY SO MUCH THAT YOU DIDN'T GIVE A FUCK HOW MUCH TIME HAD PASSED? YOU GOT SO DAMNED INVOLVED IN IT THAT IT WAS LIKE FREE-FALLING INTO A RABBIT HOLE, NO LONGER IN THIS WORLD AND MAYBE NOT EVEN IN YOUR OWN SKIN. OR MAYBE YOU'RE MORE YOURSELF THAN EVER DOWN THERE. THE RABBIT HOLE—SOMETIMES CALLED THE "ZONE"— IS WHERE YOU'RE MORE YOURSELF AND MORE ALIVE THAN ANYWHERE ELSE. SO ENJOY THE RIDE!

When you get a groove going, time flies.

DONALD FAGEN

What activities or projects throw you headfirst into the rabbit hole? When was the last time you did any of them? Describe these activities, what it felt like to engage in them, and how long it's been since you last worked on them below. If it's been a while, carve out a space to go do it next week.

It's a Great Shitty Day!

SO YOU'VE HAD A SHITTY DAY? WELL, BELIEVE IT
OR NOT, EVEN A REALLY SHITTY DAY HAS SOME GOOD STUFF
IN IT. IT'S JUST THAT YOU CAN'T SEE THE GOOD BECAUSE
YOU'RE FOCUSED ON THE SHIT. ONCE A COUPLE OF SHITTY
THINGS HAPPEN, YOU START TO SEE EVERYTHING THROUGH
THOSE SHIT-COLORED GLASSES. TAKE THOSE ICKY
GLASSES OFF AND THINK ABOUT ONE COOL THING THAT
HAPPENED TODAY. EVEN A SHITTY DAY ISN'T A
THROW-AWAY DAY BECAUSE GREAT THINGS SOMETIMES
GROW OUT OF ALL THAT SHIT.

*At the age of 18, I made up my mind to never have
another bad day in my life. I dove into a endless sea of
gratitude from which I've never emerged.*

PATCH ADAMS

Time to switch to your rose-colored glasses! Make a list of things you're grateful for. If you're in such a shitty place that you have trouble finding big things, write down small things, like the fact that you got home safely despite torrential rain. Or that there's a pint of Ben & Jerry's waiting for you in the freezer.

Blissful Blisters

Ah, bliss. I find mine hiking up mountains. Maybe you find yours at heavy metal concerts or poolside at luxury hotels. Wherever your bliss hangs out, let's be honest: Meeting up with it often isn't all rainbows and unicorns. In my case, it comes with profuse sweating, aching knees, and blisters. But the reward of those spectacular views when I get to the top far outweighs the discomfort, so it's totally worth it to me.

Close your eyes and recall a place where you found your bliss. Where was it?

What kind of difficulties did you face to get there/be there?

What made it worth the difficulties?

Draw yourself at the top of this mountain, and the path you took to get there. Label the mountain with whatever word best sums up why the trek to your bliss was worth it. Fuck yeah!

AN ADVANTAGE TO BEING FULLY PRESENT IN THE BODY IS THOSE MOMENTS WHEN WE CAN GET DOWN TO THE EXPERIENCE OF PURE BEING—OF BLISS.

E. Katherine Kerr

OUCH!

You're Hurting You!

FINDING/KEEPING LOVE, MAKING/HOLDING ONTO LOTS OF MONEY, FULFILLING A DREAM . . . WE ALL HAVE THINGS IN OUR LIFE THAT WE THINK WILL MAKE US HAPPY. IRONICALLY, THE TIGHTER YOU HOLD ONTO THOSE THINGS OR IDEAS, THE MORE UNHAPPY YOU BECOME. WHY? BECAUSE ATTACHMENT TO A DESIRED OUTCOME IS ACTUALLY DRIVEN BY FEAR. DETACHING FROM THOSE EXPECTATIONS ALLOWS YOU TO BE IN THE MOMENT AND TO ACCEPT WHATEVER MAY HAPPEN. IT'S NOT THAT YOU DON'T CARE; RATHER, YOU BECOME AN OBSERVER OF BOTH YOUR EMOTIONS AND THE EBB AND FLOW OF LIFE. AND LIKE ANYTHING WORTHWHILE, DETACHMENT IS A PRACTICE, NOT A DESTINATION.

Name something you really, really want.

_____

_____

Detachment is not that you should own nothing but that nothing should own you.

ALI IBN ABI TALIB

Why do you want the thing you really really want? What do you hope it will provide? How would you feel about yourself if you didn't get it?

Close your eyes, take a few deep breaths, and relax. Focus on the desired thing or achievement. Pretend you are watching a play about yourself wanting this. What emotions would you assign to this character? Write them down.

PUT AWAY YOUR GLOVES

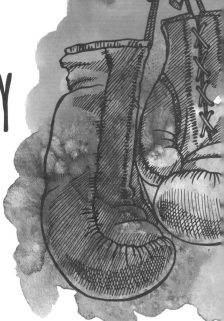

IT'S NO FUN HAVING A FIGHT WITH SOMEONE YOU CARE ABOUT. NEXT TIME, JUST APOLOGIZE, EVEN IF YOU'RE SURE YOU'RE RIGHT. FEW ARGUMENTS ARE WORTH THE PRICE OF THE RELATIONSHIP.

On the next page, write a short apology letter to someone you've had a fight with. It can be someone you argued with recently or someone you're estranged from. It's your choice whether to send it or not.

Sorry seems to be the hardest word.

ELTON JOHN

Dear,

Well,
AIN'T THAT NICE?

My friend loves to tell a joke about two southern belles, Violet and Daisy, sitting on a porch drinking mint juleps. Daisy brags about the bracelet her husband gave her on their first anniversary and the necklace he gave her on their second. Each time, Violet simply answers, "Ain't that nice." Finally, Daisy asks Violet what her husband gave her for their first anniversary, to which Violet answers, "He sent me to charm school." "Whatever for?" asks Daisy. Violet calmly responds, "So I could learn to say 'ain't that nice' instead of 'fuck you'!"

Think of all the times a person has bragged to you about something. For each brag, write the words, "Ain't That Nice" on the opposite page using colored pens or pencils. Make these words as bold and elaborate as you want. Feel free to mutter any resentments as you draw, then ultimately to let the resentments go. Ain't that nice?

*Politeness is only one half good manners and
the other half good lying.*

MARY WILSON LITTLE

SOMETIMES YA JUST GOTTA BE A FUCKING GRASSHOPPER

AESOP'S CLASSIC FABLE, "THE GRASSHOPPER AND THE ANT," IS ABOUT A GRASSHOPPER WHO SANG AND PLAYED ALL SUMMER WHILE THE FASTIDIOUS ANT PREPARED FOR WINTER. WHEN WINTER CAME, THE ANT WAS WELL STOCKED, BUT THE GRASSHOPPER WAS HUNGRY. THE ANT WOULDN'T SHARE. THE POINT IS TO WORK HARD AND PREPARE FOR THE FUTURE.

Pfft...!

SURE, IT'S IMPORTANT TO PLAN FOR TOMORROW, BUT IT SHOULDN'T BE AT THE EXPENSE OF ALL YOUR TODAYS. GO OUT AND ENJOY LIFE!

But first, put together your to-do list for the immediate future below.

Now list all of the things you're gonna do instead:

_Ha!_

Chillin' Cat Wisdom

CATS HAVE IT MADE. THEY LIE AROUND THE HOUSE ALL DAY. IN BETWEEN NAPS, THEY EAT AND GET CUDDLED AND MASSAGED. THEY MIGHT GET JAZZED UP ON CATNIP AND HAVE THEIR WAY WITH THE CAT TOYS. THEY MIGHT TEAR UP PAPERS OR MAKE 25 TRIPS TO THE TREAT CABINET. BUT THEY REALLY SPECIALIZE IN LYING AROUND.

TAKE A DAY TO PAMPER YOURSELF. SLEEP, READ A BOOK, AND MAYBE EVEN GET A MASSAGE. IN OTHER WORDS, CHILL LIKE A CAT.

How do you feel thinking about taking a "cat" day? Does it sound great, or does it seem too decadent?

What would make the perfect "cat" day for you? (After describing your perfect "cat" day, don't forget to actually take it!)

Cats don't beat themselves up about not working hard enough. They see the treadmills of human obligations for what they are—a meaningless waste of naptime.

HELEN BROWN

DOGGONE DOGGIE JOY

RUN AROUND, HOWL, JUMP UP AND DOWN, OR DANCE TO YOUR FAVORITE TUNES. (JUST DON'T PEE ON THE CARPET.)

What music do you like best when you're feeling upbeat?
Put it on now and doodle all over these pages.

FUCK AN *Organized Life*

LIFE IS MESSY, SO WHY BOTHER TRYING TO ORGANIZE IT INTO A NICE, NEAT PACKAGE? YOU'LL NEVER MANAGE. INSTEAD, JUST ORGANIZE A CLOSET OR A DRAWER. OR REARRANGE A ROOM. IT'S ACTUALLY DOABLE AND SATISFYING!

Use the grid to plan where you will put your stuff. A square can represent an inch or a foot, depending on the space you're organizing.

IN THE SCOPE OF A HAPPY LIFE,
A MESSY DESK OR AN
OVERSTUFFED COAT CLOSET IS A
TRIVIAL THING, YET . . .
GETTING RID OF CLUTTER GIVES A
DISPROPORTIONATE BOOST
TO HAPPINESS.

Gretchen Rubin

SELF-NURTURING 101:
Bean There for You

REMEMBER THAT PROJECT YOU DID IN SCHOOL WHERE YOU GREW A PLANT FROM A LIMA BEAN? WE'RE BRINGING THAT LITTLE LESSON BACK FOR A GROWN-UP PURPOSE: LEARNING TO NURTURE YOURSELF.

1. Get a lima bean.

2. Put it inside a wet paper towel.

3. Place the paper towel in a gallon-sized plastic bag, and write your name on the bag. This is now the lima bean's name, too.

4. Re-wet the paper towel as needed.

5. When the lima bean has about a one- to two-inch sprout, transfer it to a paper cup or small pot with soil.

6. Keep the lima bean plant alive. Talk to it. Call it by name. Tell it you love it. (Are you getting the metaphor here?)

On each of the leaves below, write things you can do to nurture yourself.

Nourishing yourself in a way that helps you blossom is attainable, and you are worth the effort.

DEBORAH DAY

ADVANCED SELF-NURTURING:
Me, Me, Me

YOU KICKED ASS WITH THAT LIMA BEAN PROJECT,
SO NOW YOU'RE READY FOR THE ADVANCED NURTURING
CLASS! HERE'S YOUR HOMEWORK SHEET. ANSWER
THE FOLLOWING QUESTION:

MIND:

How do you practice self-nurturing for your mind?

I'll kick it up by committing to:

BODY:

How do you practice self-nurturing for your body?

I'll kick it up by committing to:

EMOTIONS:

How do you practice self-nurturing for your emotions?

I'll kick it up by committing to:

SPIRIT:

How do you practice self-nurturing for your spirit?

I'll kick it up by committing to:

*We need to nurture ourselves.
To take a time out to refuel,
rejuvenate, and revive ourselves.*

DANA ARCURI

Give a Bug a Chance

HOW MANY SPIDERS HAVE YOU SQUASHED (OR GOTTEN SOMEONE ELSE TO SQUASH FOR YOU)? DID YOU EVER STEP ON ANTS JUST FOR THE FUN OF IT OR KILL A BEE JUST BECAUSE IT WAS FLYING NEARBY? YOU'RE NOT ALONE. A LOT OF PEOPLE DON'T GIVE A SHIT ABOUT BUGS' LIVES, AND FOR THE MOST PART, WE SURE AS HELL DON'T WANT TO SHARE SPACE WITH THEM! STILL, THEY'RE INNOCENT LIVES, AND WE WOULDN'T WANT TO BE SQUASHED IF SOME GIANT CAME ALONG AND THOUGHT WE WERE TOO CREEPY TO SHARE SPACE WITH, RIGHT? SO NEXT TIME YOU SEE A BEETLE STRUGGLING TO GET RIGHTSIDE UP OR A BEE FLOATING IN YOUR SWIMMING POOL, HAVE A LITTLE HEART FOR SOMETHING SMALLER AND MORE HELPLESS THAN YOU, AND GIVE IT A HAND—OR USE A STICK IF CREEPY CRAWLERS CREEP YOU OUT.

IF YOU TAKE THE TIME TO SHOW COMPASSION IN EVEN SMALL AND SPONTANEOUS WAYS, YOU TRANSCEND YOUR OWN BULLSHIT. IT'S WEIRDLY FREEING. ALL WE ARE SAYING IS GIVE BEES A CHANCE.

Let your freak flag fly. Color in these amazing insects!.

A person's a person
no matter how small.
DR. SEUSS

ZAP THOSE
Fucking Little
TIME ZAPPERS

DID YOU EVER THINK ABOUT HOW MUCH TIME YOU WASTE ON YOUR CELL PHONE? IT'S PROBABLY HOURS A DAY. HOW HARD WOULD IT BE TO SPEND A DAY (OKAY, MAYBE JUST HALF A DAY) APART FROM YOUR BELOVED PHONE?

Spend a day jotting down the amount of time you spend on your phone that's not for actual communication. (Round up to the nearest minute.) At the end of the day, add up all the minutes.

The next day, make a conscious decision not to read news, play games, or go on Instagram for half a day. Remember to breathe. How did you feel?

I find it refreshing to unplug from it for a while. You kind of forget how deeply you get embedded in it.

WILL WRIGHT

GRAB THAT PARTY BY THE BALLOONS

WAITING FOR SOMEONE ELSE TO THROW A PARTY OR A GET-TOGETHER CAN TAKE FOREVER. STOP WISHING FOR A FUN EVENT AND BE THE FUN STARTER BY HOSTING A PARTY. WHO NEEDS A REASON? MAKE IT A POTLUCK IF YOU DON'T WANT TO DO ALL THE COOKING.

Fill out the invitation below with a party plan.

It's a party!

WHEN:

WHERE:

WHAT:

Use this doodle page to doodle what you'd need for the perfect party. (Wine? Friends? Cakes the height of a toddler?)

I BELIEVE WHEN LIFE GIVES YOU LEMONS, YOU SHOULD MAKE LEMONADE ... AND TRY TO FIND SOMEONE WHOSE LIFE HAS GIVEN THEM VODKA, AND HAVE A PARTY.

Ron White

A Fleet of Passing Nows

HERE'S AN EXERCISE IN FUTILITY: TRY TO HANG ONTO NOW.
GO ON, TRY IT. AS SOON AS YOU HAVE A THOUGHT ABOUT
THAT MOMENT OF NOW, POOF! IT'S HISTORY. NOW IS SO
FLEETING, AND YET BEING PRESENT IS ALL ABOUT BEING
IN THE NOW. ENJOY EVERY SECOND OF NOW.

Right now, make a list of the ways you can savor the moment.

Realize deeply that the present moment is all you ever have.

ECKHART TOLLE

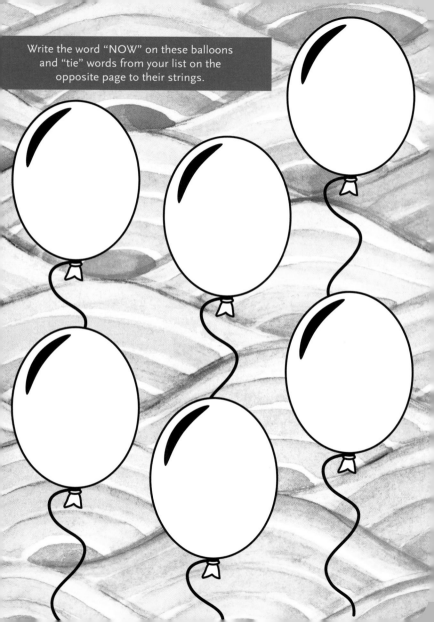

Write the word "NOW" on these balloons and "tie" words from your list on the opposite page to their strings.

SCREAMIN' DEMON PURGES

SCREAMING IS SOMETHING THAT GETS POLITE-ED OUT OF US AT A YOUNG AGE. "STOP THAT SCREAMING!" ADULTS SCREAM AT CHILDREN. (YEAH, IRONIC, ISN'T IT?) BUT SOMETIMES A GOOD SCREAM IS JUST WHAT YOU NEED TO PURGE SOME LINGERING DEMONS. IF YOUR NEIGHBORS LIVE TOO CLOSE TO YOU, SCREAMING OUT THE WINDOW AT MIDNIGHT PROBABLY ISN'T A GOOD IDEA. INSTEAD, MAKE A DATE WITH YOURSELF TO GO SCREAMING IN AN ISOLATED PLACE. INVITE OTHERS IF YOU AND THEY ARE SO INCLINED. TO MAKE IT EVEN MORE FUN, FIND A TUNNEL TO SCREAM INTO.

Draw a picture of what your purged demons look like.

JUST SCREAM! YOU
VENT, AND THE BODY
JUST FEELS GOOD AFTER
A GOOD OLD YELL.

Carol Burnett

RAIN
and Other Parade Spoilers

"ARGH! IT'S RAINING AGAIN!"
"THERE'S SO MUCH TRAFFIC!"
"MY FRIEND CANCELED DINNER!"

THERE'S NO LACK OF SHIT THAT CAN RUIN YOUR DAY
OR PISS YOU OFF. SOME STUFF YOU CAN CONTROL;
A LOT OF IT YOU CAN'T. KNOW THE DIFFERENCE
AND DON'T WASTE PRECIOUS EMOTIONAL ENERGY
ON STUFF YOU CAN'T CONTROL.

Think back to some events that altered your plans and were out of your control. How did you feel when they happened? How did you respond? If you went off the rails, what might have saved the day? How could you transcend that bullshit next time?

God grant me the serenity to accept the things I cannot change, courage to change the things I can, and wisdom to know the difference.

REINHOLD NIEBUHR

FUN AS FUCK FRIENDS

ON YOUR WAY TO INNER FUCKING PEACE, NOTHING IS MORE VALUABLE
THAN A SUPPORT GROUP. THESE ARE THE PEOPLE YOU CAN RELY ON TO
PICK YOU UP AT YOUR WORST AND REMIND YOU OF WHY YOU'RE ON YOUR
JOURNEY TO A BETTER YOU.

Who are the people you can always count on for fun and laughter?

What is it about them that you enjoy so much?

How do you contribute to the fun you have with them?

How can you contribute more to the fun?

> WHEN YOU'RE IN JAIL,
> A GOOD FRIEND WILL BE
> TRYING TO BAIL YOU OUT. A
> BEST FRIEND WILL BE IN THE
> CELL NEXT TO YOU SAYING,
> "DAMN, THAT WAS FUN."
>
> **GROUCHO MARX**

The Smell After Rain

THE SMELL OF PASTE . . . IT BRINGS ME RIGHT BACK TO
KINDERGARTEN IN AN INSTANT. TAR? I'M AT THE BEACH.
(YEAH, I KNOW THAT'S KIND OF WEIRD.) SCENTS CAN
CHANGE YOUR MOOD. FOR EXAMPLE, GRAPEFRUIT AND
OTHER CITRUS SCENTS WILL ENLIVEN YOU, WHILE
LAVENDER WILL SOOTHE RAW NERVES.

What are some of your favorite scents? Why?

Which smells trigger memories?

What memories are these?

If you're not sure, experiment with different scents and write down your findings below.

SMELL IS A POTENT WIZARD THAT TRANSPORTS YOU ACROSS
THOUSANDS OF MILES AND ALL THE YEARS YOU HAVE LIVED.

Helen Keller

Eat the Damn Cake

BEING A MARTYR ISN'T ESPECIALLY HEALTHY, AND IT'S PRETTY ANNOYING TO THE PEOPLE AROUND YOU UNLESS THEY ENJOY TAKING ADVANTAGE OF YOU. SOMETIMES IT'S JUST HEALTHIER TO EAT THE CAKE. TRUE, CAKE ISN'T REALLY HEALTHY, BUT THAT'S NOT THE POINT. WE COULD BE TALKING ABOUT TAKING A DAY OFF. OR ANYTHING ELSE YOU DEPRIVE YOURSELF OF. SO JUST EAT THE DAMN CAKE ALREADY!

Those who refuse to drink are always thirsty.

MARTY RUBIN

I deprive myself of:
_____

I'm afraid that if I didn't deprive myself of this, this might happen:

_____

_____

I got this idea from:
_____

I can change this story by:

_____

_____

I deprive myself of:
_____

I'm afraid that if I didn't deprive myself of this, this might happen:

_____

_____

_____

I got this idea from:
_____

I can change this story by:

_____

_____

GET YOURSELF COMMITTED

YOU PROBABLY HAVE A SHITLOAD OF COMMIT-MENTS. WHERE IN ALL THAT IS YOUR COMMITMENT TO YOURSELF? PICK A SPECIFIC TIME EVERY WEEK THAT IS JUST YOURS—NO EXCEPTIONS. (YOU'D DO IT FOR SOMEONE ELSE, WOULDN'T YOU?) IT CAN BE AS LITTLE AS ONE HOUR. USE THAT TIME TO DO SOMETHING FUN OR TO GET MOVING ON A DREAM YOU'VE HAD, LIKE WRITING A NOVEL, PAINTING, GO-ING TO THE PARK, GETTING A MANICURE—YOU GET THE IDEA. IT CAN BE THE SAME THING OR SOMETHING DIFFERENT EACH WEEK.

CONTRACT WITH MYSELF

I commit to dedicating every
_____
DAY

at _____ to ME.
TIME

Signed,

_____

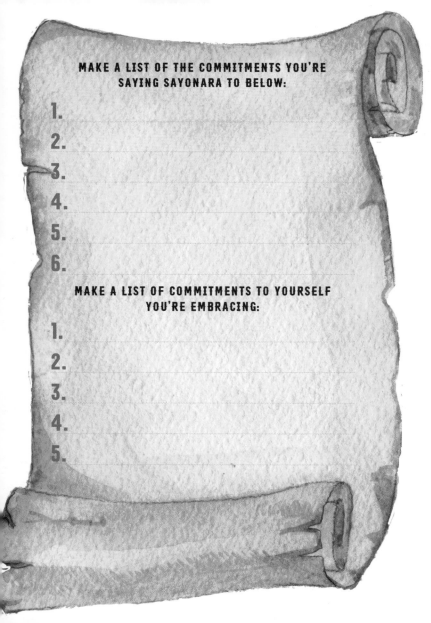

MAKE A LIST OF THE COMMITMENTS YOU'RE SAYING SAYONARA TO BELOW:

1.

2.

3.

4.

5.

6.

MAKE A LIST OF COMMITMENTS TO YOURSELF YOU'RE EMBRACING:

1.

2.

3.

4.

5.

TWISTERS AND "OH SHIT!" MOMENTS

SUDDENLY, SOME UNEXPECTED, URGENT ISSUE SMACKS YOU UPSIDE THE HEAD. DO YOU FRANTICALLY YELL "OH SHIT!" AND TURN INTO A TORNADO, RUNNING AROUND REACTIVELY AND SWEEPING UP EVERYTHING (AND EVERYONE) IN YOUR PATH? STOP! TAKE A DEEP BREATH AND CENTER YOURSELF BEFORE TAKING ACTION. BY SLOWING DOWN AND BREATHING, YOU'LL HAVE A CLEARER HEAD AND BE ABLE TO MAKE BETTER DECISIONS.

Draw a face on the tornado on the opposite page. Draw all the stuff that gets swept up into the chaos. Don't forget your family and pets.

I took a deep breath and listened to the old bray of my heart. I am. I am. I am.

SYLVIA PLATH

A Taste of
the Sky

AND ONCE YOU HAVE TASTED FLIGHT YOU WILL WALK THE EARTH WITH YOUR EYES TURNED SKYWARD.

John H. Secondari

What amazing thing have you experienced that you're itching to do again?

When is the last time you did it?

Make a plan to experience it, or something you hope will feel similarly incredible, again:

Give Up GIVING A FUCK What Others THINK OF YOU

SOME PEOPLE ARE GONNA LIKE YOU. SOME PEOPLE AREN'T. AVOID THE DISAPPOINTMENT AND THE ATTEMPTED PEOPLE-PLEASING CONTORTIONS BY FINDING YOUR TRUE WORTH FROM WITHIN.

I'm good enough, I'm smart enough, and doggone it, people like me.

AL FRANKEN *as* **STUART SMALLEY**

HERE ARE ALL THE THINGS I LIKE ABOUT MYSELF:

Exit Out the Window

YOU CAN'T AVOID ENDINGS. EVEN THIS BOOK HAS
TO END NOW. BUT IT'S TRUE THAT THE END OF ONE
THING IS THE BEGINNING OF ANOTHER. NOW YOU HAVE
SOME TOOLS YOU CAN USE TO TRANSCEND YOUR
BULLSHIT AND FIND INNER FUCKING PEACE. OR TO
JIMMY THE WINDOW. REMEMBER THAT IT'S NOT
ABOUT DOING ANYTHING PERFECTLY.
IT'S ABOUT PRACTICE.

Which tools from this book are you likely to use?

Which ones seem challenging, but you might try them anyway?

"HOW DO YOU GET TO CARNEGIE HALL?"
"PRACTICE, PRACTICE, PRACTICE!"

E. E. Kenyon

Cynthia Scher is a writer by profession and an avid journaler. The author of two other journal books, *This Time Next Year: 365 Days of Exploration* and *Girls' World: A Journal of Awesome Stuff for Girls*, she has also run numerous meditative writing workshops, as well as other types of personal development classes. Cynthia earned her master's degree in transpersonal psychology and her bachelor's degree in journalism. After years of working on her own inner peace, she has found that the key is to f*ck perfection and stop trying to fit into the round circle. Today, she embraces her irreverence, humor, and potty mouth and is way, way more peaceful.